CAN I *Know*
GOD'S WILL?

The Crucial Questions Series
By R. C. Sproul

CRUCIAL
QUESTIONS
No. 4

CAN I *Know*
GOD'S WILL?

R.C. SPROUL

Reformation Trust
PUBLISHING

A DIVISION OF LIGONIER MINISTRIES · ORLANDO, FLORIDA

Can I Know God's Will?

© 1984, 1999, 2009 by R. C. Sproul

Previously published as *God's Will and the Christian* (1984) and as part of *Following Christ* (1991) by Tyndale House Publishers, and as *Can I Know God's Will?* by Ligonier Ministries (1999).

Published by Reformation Trust
a division of Ligonier Ministries
400 Technology Park, Lake Mary, FL 32746
www.Ligonier.org   www.ReformationTrust.com

Printed in the United States of America

Cover design: Gearbox Studios
Interior design and typeset: Katherine Lloyd, The DESK, Colorado Springs

Unless otherwise noted, Scripture quotations are from The Holy Bible, English Standard Version®, copyright © 2001 by Crossway Bibles, a publishing ministry of Good News Publishers. Used by permission. All rights reserved.

Scripture quotations marked RSV are taken from the Revised Standard Version of the Bible, copyright 1952 (2nd edition, 1971) by the Division of Christian Education of the National Council of the Churches of Christ in the United States of America. Used by permission. All rights reserved.

Scripture quotations marked KJV are from The Holy Bible, King James Version.

Library of Congress Cataloging-in-Publication Data
Sproul, R. C. (Robert Charles), 1939-
    [God's will and the Christian]
    Can I know God's will? / R.C. Sproul.
        p. cm. -- (The crucial questions series)
    First published as: God's will and the Christian. 1984. Following Christ. Wheaton, Ill. : Tyndale House Publishers, c1991. Can I know God's Will? Ligonier Ministries, 1999.
    ISBN 978-1-56769-179-5
    1. Providence and government of God--Christianity. 2. God (Christianity)--Will. I. Sproul, R. C. (Robert Charles), 1939- Following Christ. II. Title.
    BT135.S745 2009
    248.4--dc22

                                        2009018820

Contents

Chapter One

THE MEANING
OF GOD'S WILL

Lost in Wonderland, Alice came to a fork in the road. Icy panic stung her as she stood frozen by indecision. She lifted her eyes toward heaven, looking for guidance. Her eyes did not find God, only the Cheshire cat leering at her from his perch in the tree above.

"Which way should I go?" Alice blurted.

"That depends," said the cat, fixing a sardonic smile on the confused girl.

"On what?" Alice managed to reply.

"It depends on your destination. Where are you going?" the cat asked.

"I don't know," Alice stammered.

"Then," said the cat, his grin spreading wider, "it doesn't matter which way you go."

The destination matters to the Christian. We are a pilgrim people. Though we do not wander in a wilderness in route to the Promised Land, we seek a better country, an eternal city whose builder and maker is God. Someday He will take us home to His kingdom.

So the ultimate destination is clear. We are certain that there is a glorious future for the people of God. However, what of tomorrow? We feel anxious about the immediate future, just as unbelievers do. The specifics of our personal futures are unknown to us. Like children we ask: "Will I be happy? Will I be rich? What will happen to me?" We must walk by faith rather than by sight.

As long as there have been people, there have been soothsayers and wizards exploiting our anxieties. If prostitution is the world's oldest profession, surely fortune-telling is the second oldest. "Tell me of tomorrow" is the plea of the stock market speculator, the competitive businessman, the sports forecaster, and the young couple in love. The student asks, "Will I graduate?" The manager muses, "Will I be promoted?" The person in the doctor's waiting room clenches his hands and asks, "Is it cancer or indigestion?" People have examined lizard entrails, snakeskins, the bones of owls, the Ouija board, the daily horoscope, and the predictions of sports handicappers—all to gain a small margin of insurance against an unknown future.

The Christian feels the same curiosity, but frames the question differently. He asks: "What is the will of God for my life?" To search for the will of God can be an exercise in piety or impiety, an act of humble submission or outrageous arrogance—depending on what will of God we seek. To try to look behind the veil at what God has not been pleased to reveal is to tamper with holy things that are out of bounds. John Calvin said that when God "closes his holy mouth," we should desist from inquiry (*Commentaries on the Epistle of Paul the Apostle to the Romans*, trans. and ed. John Owen [reprint, Grand Rapids, Mich.: Baker Book House. 2003], 354).

On the other hand, God delights to hear the prayers of His people when they individually ask, "Lord, what do you want me to do?" The Christian pursues God, looking for His marching orders, seeking to know what course of action is pleasing to Him. This search for the will of God is a holy quest—a pursuit that is to be undertaken with vigor by the godly person.

The Biblical Meaning of the Will of God

We yearn for simple answers to difficult questions. We want clarity. We desire to cut through the entanglements to the heart of the question. Sometimes the answers are *simple* enough in themselves, but the process of finding them is laborious and confusing. Sometimes the answers are *simplistic*, giving us temporary relief from the pressures and the burdens of confusing questions.

However, there is a profound difference between the *simple* answer and the *simplistic* answer. The simple answer is correct; it accounts for all the data found in the complex problem. It is clear and can be easily grasped in its fullness. It abides, being able to stand the test of rigorous questioning. The simplistic answer is a counterfeit. On the surface it appears to be the genuine article, but under closer scrutiny it yields its bogus flaws. The simplistic answer may account for some of the data but not all of it. It remains fuzzy. Worst of all, it does not abide; it fails the test of deeper questioning. It does not satisfy in the long haul.

One of the most excruciating questions in theology is, "Why did Adam fall?" The simplistic answer, commonly heard, is that Adam fell by his own free will. Such an answer is satisfying until we probe the question more deeply. Suppose we ask: "How could a righteous creature made by a perfect Creator sin? How could Adam make an evil choice while possessing no prior inclination or disposition to evil? Was he simply deceived or coerced by Satan? If so, why would Adam then be blameworthy?" If he was merely deceived, then the fault is all Satan's. If he was coerced, then it was not a free choice. If he sinned because he had a prior desire or inclination to sin, then we must ask: "What was the source of his evil desire? Did God put it there?" If so, then we cast a shadow on the integrity of the Creator.

Perhaps the simplest way to expose the weak character of the simplistic answer that Adam fell by his own free will is to ask our question another way: "Why did Adam exercise his own free will to sin?" It simply won't do to answer, "Because he chose to." This answer is a mere repetition of the question in a declarative form.

I would like to offer a simple answer to the difficult question of Adam's fall, but I simply can't. The only response I can give to the question is that I don't know the answer.

Some readers will surely chasten me at this point by

saying to themselves: "I know the answer! Adam fell because it was the will of God."

I immediately ask: "In what sense was Adam's fall the will of God? Did God *force* Adam to fall and then punish him for doing what he had no power to avoid?" To ask such an impious question is to answer it. Certainly the fall must have been the "will of God" in some sense, but the crucial question remains, "In what sense?"

So here we are, pressed squarely against a biting question that involves the matter of the will of God. We want to know how the will of God worked in Adam's life; but more personally, we want to know how the will of God works in our own lives.

When questions are difficult and complex, it is a good rule to collect as much data about them as possible. The more clues the detective has to work with, the easier it usually is to solve the crime (note the word *usually*). Sometimes the detective suffers from too many clues, which only serve to compound the difficulty of the solution. The corporate executive faced with major decision-making responsibilities knows the importance of sufficient data- and record-keeping. His maxim may be: "If you have enough data, the decisions jump out at you." Again we must add the qualifier *usually*. Sometimes the data are so complex that they jump out like screaming banshees, defying our ability to sort through them all.

I emphasize the point of data, complexity, and simplicity because the biblical meaning of the will of God is a very complicated matter. To approach it simplistically is to invite disaster. At times, wrestling with the complexities of the biblical concept of the will of God can give us an Excedrin headache. Yet ours is a holy quest, a pursuit that is worth a few headaches along the way. But we must guard against proceeding in a simplistic way, lest we change the holy quest into an unholy presumption.

We note at the outset that the Bible speaks of the "will of God" in more than one way. This is the key problem that complicates our quest and serves as a warning against simplistic solutions. In the New Testament, there are two Greek words that can be and have been translated by the English word *will.* It would seem that all we need is to identify precisely the meanings of the two words and check out the Greek text every time we see the word *will,* and our problems will be solved. Alas, it doesn't work that way. The plot thickens when we discover that each of the two Greek words has several nuances of meaning. Simply checking the Greek text for word usage is not enough to solve our difficulty.

However, finding the meanings of the Greek words is a

helpful starting place. Let's examine the two words briefly to see whether they shed any light on our quest. The words are *boule* and *thelema*.

The term *boule* has its roots in an ancient verb that means a "rational and conscious desire," as opposed to *thelema,* meaning "an impulsive or unconscious desire." The ancient subtle distinction was between rational desire and impulsive desire. As the Greek language developed, however, this distinction was softened, and eventually the words became used at times as synonyms, with authors switching from one to the other for purposes of stylistic change.

In the New Testament, *boule* usually refers to a plan based on careful deliberation; it is used most often with respect to the counsel of God. *Boule* frequently indicates God's providential plan, which is predetermined and inflexible. Luke is fond of using it this way, as we read in the book of Acts: "This Jesus, delivered up according to the definite plan [*boule*] and foreknowledge of God, you crucified and killed by the hands of lawless men" (Acts 2:23).

Here the resolute decree of God is in view, which no human action can set aside. God's plan is impregnable; His "will" is unalterable.

The word *thelema* is rich in its diversity of meanings. It refers to what is agreeable, what is desired, what is intended, what is chosen, or what is commanded. Here we have the notions of consent, desire, purpose, resolution, and command. The force of the various meanings is determined by the context in which *thelema* appears.

The Decretive Will of God

Theologians describe as the "decretive will of God" that will by which God decrees things to come to pass according to His supreme sovereignty. This is also sometimes called "God's sovereign efficacious will"; by it, God brings to pass whatsoever He wills. When God sovereignly decrees something in this sense, nothing can prevent it from coming to pass.

When God commanded the light to shine, the darkness had no power to resist the command. The "lights" came on. God did not persuade the light to shine. He did not negotiate with elemental powers to form a universe. He did not achieve a plan of redemption by trial and error; the cross was not a cosmic accident exploited by the Deity. These things were decreed absolutely. Their effects were efficacious (producing the desired result) because their causes were sovereignly decreed.

A serious danger faces those who restrict the meaning of

the will of God to the sovereign will. We hear the Muslim cry, "It is the will of Allah." We slip at times into a deterministic view of life that says, "*Que será, sera,*" or "What will be, will be." In so doing, we embrace a sub-Christian form of fatalism, as if God willed everything that happened in such a way as to eliminate human choices.

Classical theologians insist on the reality of man's will in acting, choosing, and responding. God works His plan through *means*, via the real choices of willing and acting creatures. There are secondary as well as primary causes. To deny this is to embrace a kind of determinism that eliminates human freedom and dignity.

Yet there is a God who is sovereign, whose will is greater than ours. His will restricts my will. My will cannot restrict His will. When He decrees something sovereignly, it will come to pass—whether I like it or not, whether I choose it or not. He is sovereign. I am subordinate.

The Preceptive Will of God

When the Bible speaks of the will of God, it does not always mean the decretive will of God. The decretive will of God cannot be broken or disobeyed. It will come to pass. On the other hand, there is a will that can be broken: "the preceptive will of God." It can be disobeyed. Indeed, it is broken and disobeyed every day by each one of us.

The preceptive will of God is found in His law. The precepts, statutes, and commandments that He delivers to His people make up the preceptive will. They express and reveal to us what is right and proper for us to do. The preceptive will is God's rule of righteousness for our lives. By this rule we are governed.

It is the will of God that we not sin. It is the will of God that we have no other gods before Him; that we love our neighbor as we love ourselves; that we refrain from stealing, coveting, and committing adultery. Yet the world is filled with idolatry, hatred, thievery, covetousness, and adultery. The will of God is violated whenever His law is broken.

One of the great tragedies of contemporary Christendom is the preoccupation of so many Christians with the secret decretive will of God to the exclusion and neglect of the preceptive will. We want to peek behind the veil, to catch a glimpse of our personal future. We seem more concerned with our horoscope than with our obedience, more concerned with what the stars in their courses are doing than with what we are doing.

With respect to God's sovereign will, we assume we are passive. With respect to His preceptive will, we know that we are active and therefore responsible and accountable. It is easier to engage in ungodly prying into the secret counsel of God than to apply ourselves to the practice of godliness. We can flee to the safety of the sovereign will and try to pass off our sin to God, laying the burden and responsibility of it on His unchanging will. Such characterizes the spirit of antichrist, the spirit of lawlessness or antinomianism, that despises God's law and ignores His precepts.

Protestants are particularly vulnerable to this distortion. We seek refuge in our precious doctrine of justification by faith alone, forgetting that the very doctrine is to be a catalyst for the pursuit of righteousness and obedience to the preceptive will of God.

Biblical Righteousness

Habakkuk's famous statement, "the just shall live by his faith" (Hab. 2:4, KJV), is found three times in the New Testament. It has become a slogan of evangelical Protestantism, whose emphasis has been on the doctrine of justification by faith alone. This slogan, containing a hint of the essence of the Christian life, has its focal point in the biblical concept of righteousness.

One of Jesus' most disturbing comments was the statement, "Unless your righteousness exceeds that of the scribes and Pharisees, you will never enter the kingdom of heaven" (Matt. 5:20). It is easy for us to assume that Jesus meant that our righteousness must be of a higher sort than that characterized by men who were hypocrites. The image that we have of scribes and Pharisees from the New Testament period is that of unscrupulous, ruthless practitioners of religious deceit. We must bear in mind, however, that the Pharisees as a group were men historically committed to a very lofty level of righteous living. Yet Jesus tells us that our righteousness must exceed theirs. What did He mean?

When we consider the biblical notion of righteousness, we are dealing with a matter that touches virtually every plane of theology. In the first place, there is the righteousness of God, by which all standards of rightness and wrongness are to be measured. God's character is the ultimate foundation and model of righteousness. In the Old Testament, righteousness becomes defined in terms of obedience to the commandments delivered by God, who Himself is altogether righteous. Those commands include not only precepts of human behavior with respect to our fellow human beings, but also matters of a liturgical and ceremonial nature.

In Old Testament Israel and among the New Testament

Pharisees, liturgical righteousness was substituted for authentic righteousness. That is to say, men became satisfied with obeying the rituals of the religious community rather than fulfilling the broader implications of the law. For example, Jesus rebuked the Pharisees for tithing their mint and cumin while omitting the weightier matters of the law: justice and mercy. Jesus indicated that the Pharisees were correct in giving their tithes, but were incorrect in assuming that the liturgical exercises had completed the requirements of the law. Here, liturgical righteousness had become a substitute for true and full obedience.

Within the evangelical world, *righteousness* is a rare word indeed. We speak of morality, spirituality, and piety. Seldom, however, do we speak of righteousness. Yet the goal of our redemption is not piety or spirituality but righteousness. Spirituality in the New Testament sense is a means to the end of righteousness. Being spiritual means that we are exercising the spiritual graces given by God to mold us after the image of His Son. The disciplines of prayer, Bible study, church fellowship, witnessing, and the like are not ends in themselves, but are designed to assist us in living righteously. We are stunted in our growth if we assume that the end of the Christian life is spirituality.

Spiritual concerns are but the beginning of our walk

with God. We must beware of the subtle danger of thinking that spirituality completes the requirements of Christ. To fall into such a trap—the trap of the Pharisees—is to substitute liturgical or ritualistic practices for authentic righteousness. By all means we are to pray and to study the Bible, and to bear witness in evangelism. However, we must never, at any point in our lives, rest from our pursuit of righteousness.

In justification we become righteous in the sight of God by means of the cloak of Christ's righteousness. However, as soon as we are justified, our lives must give evidence of the personal righteousness that flows out of our justification. It is interesting to me that the whole biblical concept of righteousness is contained in one Greek word, *dikaios*. That same Greek word is used to refer, in the first instance, to the righteousness of God; in the second instance, to what we call justification; and in the third instance, to the righteousness of life. Thus, from beginning to end—from the nature of God to the destiny of man—our human duty remains the same—a call to righteousness.

True righteousness must never be confused with self-righteousness. Since our righteousness proceeds from our justification, which is based on the righteousness of Christ alone, we must never be deluded into thinking that our works of righteousness have any merit of their own. Yet as Protestants, zealously maintaining our doctrine of justification by faith alone, we must be ever mindful that the justification that is by faith alone is never *by a faith that is alone.* True faith manifests itself in righteousness exceeding that of the Pharisees and the scribes, for it is concerned with the weightier matters of the law: justice and mercy.

We are called to bear witness to the righteousness of God in every area of life—from our prayer closets to our courtrooms, from our pews to our marketplaces. The top priority of Jesus is that we seek first the kingdom of God and His righteousness. All other things will be added to that.

An Allergy to Restraint

"Everybody do your own thing." This cliché from the sixties characterizes the spirit of our age. Increasingly freedom is being equated with the inalienable right to do whatever you please. It carries with it a built-in allergy to laws that restrain, whether they be the laws of God or the laws of men.

This pervasive anti-law, or antinomian, attitude is reminiscent of the biblical epoch that provoked God's judgment because "everyone did what was right in his own eyes" (Judg. 17:6). The secular world reflects this attitude in the statement, "Government can't legislate morality." Morality is seen as a private matter, outside the domain of the state and even of the church.

A shift has occurred in word meaning so subtle that many have missed it. The original intent of the concept, "You cannot legislate morality," was to convey the idea that passing a law prohibiting a particular kind of activity would not necessarily eliminate such activity. The point of the phrase was that laws do not *ipso facto* produce obedience to those laws. In fact, on some occasions, the legal prohibition of certain practices has incited only greater violation of established law. The prohibition of alcoholic beverages is an example.

The contemporary interpretation of legislating morality differs from the original intent. Instead of saying that government *cannot* legislate morality, it says government *may not* legislate morality. That means government should stay out of moral issues such as the regulation of abortion, deviant sexual practices, marriage and divorce, and so on, since morality is a matter of conscience in the private sector. For government to legislate in these areas is often viewed as an invasion of privacy by the state, representing a denial of basic freedoms for the individual.

If we take this kind of thinking to its logical conclusion, we leave the government with little to do. If government may not legislate morality, its activity will be restricted to determining the colors of the state flag, the state flower, and perhaps the state bird. (However, even questions of flowers and birds may be deemed "moral," as they touch on ecological issues, which are ultimately moral in character.) The vast majority of matters that concern legislation are, in fact, of a decidedly moral character. The regulation of murder, theft, and civil rights is a moral matter. How a person operates his automobile on the highway is a moral issue since it touches on the well-being of fellow travelers.

Questions relating to the legalization of marijuana often focus on the fact that a majority of certain age groups are violating the law. The argument goes like this: Since disobedience is so widespread, doesn't this indicate that the law is bad? Such a conclusion is a blatant non sequitur. Whether or not marijuana should be decriminalized should not be determined by levels of civil disobedience.

The point is that a vast number of Americans reflect an antinomian spirit regarding marijuana. Such disobedience is hardly motivated by noble aspirations to a higher ethic suppressed by a tyrannical government. Here the law is broken as a matter of convenience and physical appetite.

Within the church, the same spirit of antinomianism has prevailed too often. Pope Benedict XVI faces the embarrassing legacy of his predecessors as he tries to explain to the world why a majority of his American adherents tell the pollsters they practice artificial means of birth control when a papal encyclical explicitly forbids such methods. One must ask how people can confess their belief in an "infallible" leader of their church and at the same time obstinately refuse to submit to that leader.

Within the Protestant churches, individuals frequently become irate when called to moral accountability. They often declare that the church has no right to intrude into their private lives. They say this in spite of the fact that in their membership vows, they publicly committed themselves to submit to the moral oversight of the church.

Antinomianism should be more rare in the evangelical Christian community than anywhere else. Sadly, the facts do not fit the theory. So blasé is the typical "evangelical" toward the law of God that the prophecies of doom that Rome thundered at Martin Luther are beginning to come true. Some "evangelicals" are indeed using justification by faith alone as a license to sin; these can be deemed properly only as pseudo-evangelicals. Anyone who has the most rudimentary understanding of justification by faith knows that authentic faith always manifests itself in a zeal for obedience. No earnest Christian can ever have a cavalier attitude toward the law of God. Though obedience to such laws does not bring justification, the justified person will surely endeavor to obey them.

To be sure, there are times when the commandments of men are on a collision course with the laws of God. In those instances, Christians not only *may* disobey men, but *must* disobey men. I am not talking here of isolated moral issues but of attitudes. Christians must be particularly careful in this era of antinomianism not to get caught up in the spirit of the age. We are not free to do what is right in our own eyes. We are called to do what is right in His eyes.

Freedom should not be confused with autonomy. As long as evil exists in the world, the moral restraint of law is necessary. It is an act of grace by which God institutes government, which exists to restrain the evildoer. It exists to protect the innocent and the righteous. The righteous are called to support it as much as they possibly can without compromising their obedience to God.

God's Will of Disposition

While we understand that the decretive will and the preceptive will of God are part of His overall will, other aspects of the mystery of His sovereignty remain. One such aspect is "the will of disposition." It is tied up with the ability of man to disobey God's preceptive will.

This aspect of the will of God refers to what is pleasing and agreeable to God. It expresses something of the attitude of God to His creatures. Some things are "well pleasing in his sight," while other things are said to grieve Him. He may allow (but not via moral permission) wicked things to transpire, but He is by no means pleased by them.

To illustrate how these differing aspects of the will of God come into play in biblical interpretation, let us examine the verse that says the Lord is "not willing that any should perish" (2 Peter 3:9, KJV). Which of the above-mentioned meanings of *will* fits this text? How is the meaning of the text changed by the application of the nuances?

Try first the decretive will. The verse would then mean, "God is not willing in a sovereign decretive sense that any should perish." The implication would then be that nobody perishes. This verse would be a proof text for universalism, with its view that hell is utterly vacant of people.

The second option is that God is not willing in a preceptive way that any should perish. This would mean that God does not *allow* people to perish in the sense that He grants His moral permission. This obviously does not fit the context of the passage.

The third option makes sense. God is not willing in the sense that He is not inwardly disposed to, or delighted by, people's perishing. Elsewhere, Scripture teaches that God takes no delight in the death of the wicked. He may decree what He does not enjoy; that is, He may distribute justice to wicked offenders. He is pleased when justice is maintained and righteousness is honored, even though He takes no personal pleasure in the application of such punishment.

A human analogy may be seen in our law courts. A judge, in the interest of justice, may sentence a criminal to prison and at the same time inwardly grieve for the guilty man. His disposition may be *for* the man but against the crime.

However, God is not merely a human judge, working under the constraints of the criminal justice system. God is sovereign—He can do what He pleases. If He is not pleased or willing that any should perish, why then does He not exercise His decretive will accordingly? How can there be a hiatus between God's decretive will and His will of disposition?

All things being equal, God does desire that no one should perish. But all things are not equal. Sin is real. Sin violates God's holiness and righteousness. God also is not willing that sin should go unpunished. He desires as well that His holiness should be vindicated. It is dangerous to speak of a conflict of interests or of a clash of desires within God. Yet, in a certain sense, we must. He wills the obedience of His creatures. He wills the well-being of His creatures. There is a symmetry of relationship ultimately between obedience and well-being. The obedient child will never perish. Those who obey God's preceptive will enjoy the benefits of His will of disposition. When the preceptive will is violated, things are no longer equal. Now God requires punishment while not particularly enjoying the application of it.

Yet does this not beg the ultimate question? Where does the decretive will fit in? Could not God originally have decreed that no one ever would be *able* to sin, thus ensuring an eternal harmony among all elements of His will: decretive, preceptive, and dispositional?

Often the answer to this question is superficial. Appeals are made to the free will of man, as if by magic man's free will could explain the dilemma. We are told that the only way God could have created a universe guaranteed to be free from sin would have been to make creatures without free will. It is then argued that these creatures would have been nothing more than puppets and would have lacked humanity, being devoid of the power or ability to sin. If that is the case, then what does it suggest about the state of our existence in heaven? We are promised that when our redemption is complete, sin will be no more. We will still have an ability to choose, but our disposition will be so inclined toward righteousness that we will, in fact, never choose evil. If this will be possible in heaven after redemption, why could it not have been possible *before* the fall?

The Bible gives no clear answer to this thorny question. We are told that God created people who, for better or for worse, have the ability to sin. We also know from Scripture that there is no shadow of turning in the character of God, and that all of His works are clothed in righteousness. That He chose to create man the way He did is mysterious, but we must assume, given the knowledge we have, that God's plan was good. Any conflict that arises between His commandments to us, His desire that we should obey Him, and our failure to comply does not destroy His sovereignty.

God's Secret and Revealed Will

We have already distinguished among the three types of the will of God: His decretive will, His preceptive will, and His will of disposition. Another distinction must be established between what is called God's *secret,* or hidden, will and His *revealed* will. This secret will of God is subsumed under the decretive will because, for the most part, it remains undisclosed to us. There is a limit to the revelation God has made of Himself. We know certain things about God's decretive will that He has been pleased to set forth for our information in Holy Scripture. But because we are finite creatures, we do not comprehend the total dimension of divine knowledge or the divine plan. As the Scriptures teach, the secret things belong to the Lord, but that which He has revealed belongs to us and to our children forever (Deut. 29:29).

Protestant theologians have made use of the distinction between the hidden God (*Deus obsconditus*) and the revealed God (*Deus revelatus*). This distinction is valuable and indeed necessary when we realize that not all that can be known of God has been revealed to us. There is a sense in which God remains hidden from us, insofar as He has not been pleased to reveal all there is to know about Him. However, this distinction is fraught with peril since some have found within it a conflict between two kinds of gods. A god who reveals his character to be one thing, but who is secretly contrary to that revealed character, would be a supreme hypocrite.

If we say that God has no secret will and proposes to do only what He commands and nothing more, then we would perceive God as one whose desires and plans are constantly thwarted by the harassment of human beings. Such a god would be impotent, and no god at all.

If we distinguish between the secret aspect of God and the revealed aspect of God, we must hold these as parts of the whole, not as contradictions. That is to say, what God has revealed about Himself is trustworthy. Our knowledge is partial, but it is true as far as it goes. What belongs to the secret counsel of God does not contradict the character of God that has been revealed to us.

The distinction of God's revealed will and hidden will raises a practical problem: the question of whether or not it is possible for a Christian to act in harmony with God's decretive (hidden) will and at the same time work against His preceptive will.

We must admit that such a possibility exists—in a sense. For example, it was in God's decretive will and by His determinate counsel that Jesus Christ was condemned to die on the cross. The divine purpose, of course, was to secure the redemption of God's people. However, that purpose was hidden from the view of men who sat in judgment over Jesus. When Pontius Pilate delivered Jesus to be crucified, Pilate acted against the preceptive will of God but in harmony with the decretive will of God. Does this make nonsense of God's preceptive will? God forbid. What it does is bear witness to the transcendent power of God to work His purposes sovereignly in spite of, and by means of, the evil acts of men.

Consider the story of Joseph, whose brothers, out of jealousy and greed, sold their innocent brother into slavery in Egypt. At their reunion years later, and upon the brothers' confession of sin, Joseph replied, "You meant evil against me, but God meant it for good" (Gen. 50:20). Here is the inscrutable majesty of God's providence. God made use of human evil in bringing to pass His purposes for Joseph and for the Jewish nation. Joseph's brothers were guilty of willful and malicious sin. By directly violating the preceptive will of God, they sinned against their brother and against God. Yet in their sin, God's secret counsel was brought to pass, and God brought redemption through it.

What if Joseph's brothers had been obedient? Joseph would not have been sold into slavery; he would not have been taken to Egypt; he would not have been sent to prison, from which he was called to interpret a dream. What if Joseph had not become prime minister? What would have become the historical reason for the brothers' settling in Egypt? There would have been no Jewish settlement in Egypt, no Moses, no exodus from Egypt, no law, no prophets, no Christ, no salvation.

Can we, therefore, conclude that the sins of Joseph's brothers were, in fact, virtues in disguise? Not at all. Their sin was sin, a clear violation of the preceptive will of God, for which they were held responsible and judged to be guilty. But God brought good out of evil. This reflects neither a contradiction in God's character nor a contradiction between His precepts and His decrees. Rather it calls attention to the transcendent power of His sovereignty.

Is it possible for us in this day and age to obey the preceptive will of God and yet be in conflict with the secret will of God? Of course this is possible. It may be the will of God, for example, that He use a foreign nation to chastise the United States for sinning against God. It may be in the plan of God to have the people of the United States brought under judgment through the aggressive invasion of Russia. In terms of God's inscrutable will, He could be, for purposes of judgment, "on the side of the Russians." Yet at the same time, it would remain the duty of the civil magistrate of the American nation to resist the transgression of our borders by a conquering nation.

We have a parallel in the history of Israel, where God used the Babylonians as a rod to chastise His people Israel. In that situation, it would have been perfectly proper for the civil magistrate of Israel to have resisted the wicked invasion of the Babylonians. In so doing, the Israelites would have been, in effect, resisting the decretive will of God. The book of Habakkuk wrestles with the severe problem of God's use of the evil inclinations of men to bring judgment on His people. This is not to suggest that God favored the Babylonians. He made it clear that judgment would fall on them also, but He first made use of their evil inclinations in order to bring a corrective discipline to His own people.

Knowing the Will of God for Our Lives

Pursuing knowledge of the will of God is not an abstract science designed to titillate the intellect or to convey the kind of knowledge that "puffs up" but fails to edify. An understanding of the will of God is desperately important for every Christian seeking to live a life that is pleasing to his or her Creator. It is a very practical thing for us to know what God wants for our lives. A Christian asks: "What are my marching orders? What should my role be in contributing to the establishment of the kingdom of God? What does God want me to do with my life?" It is inconceivable that a Christian could live for very long without coming face-to-face with these gripping questions.

Having been a Christian for some fifty years, with the

study of theology my main vocational pursuit, I find the practical question of the will of God pressing on my mind quite frequently. I doubt a fortnight passes that I am not seriously engaged by the question of whether I am doing what God wants me to do at this point in my life. The question haunts and beckons all of us. It demands resolution, and so we must ask ourselves, "How do we know the will of God for our lives?"

The practical question of how we know the will of God for our lives cannot be solved with any degree of accuracy unless we have some prior understanding of the will of God in general. Without the distinctions that we have made, our pursuit of the will of God can plunge us into hopeless confusion and consternation. When we seek the will of God, we must first ask ourselves which will we are seeking to discover.

If our quest is to penetrate the hidden aspects of His will, then we have embarked on a fool's errand. We are trying the impossible and chasing the untouchable. Such a quest is not only an act of foolishness, but also an act of presumption. There is a very real sense in which the secret will of the secret counsel of God is none of our business and is off limits to our speculative investigations.

Untold evils have been perpetrated on God's people by

unscrupulous theologians who have sought to correct or to supplant the clear and plain teaching of sacred Scripture by doctrines and theories based on speculation alone. The business of searching out the mind of God where God has remained silent is dangerous business indeed. Luther put it this way: "We must keep in view his word and leave alone his inscrutable will; for it is by his word and not by his inscrutable will that we must be guided."

Christians are permitted, in a sense, to attempt to discern the will of God by means of illumination by the Holy Spirit and by confirmation through circumstances that we are doing the right thing. However, as we will discover, the search for providential guidance must always be subordinate to our study of the revealed will of God. In our search, we must also come to terms with the dynamic tensions created by the concept of man's will *versus* predestination. Before our inquiry can lead us into such practical avenues as occupation and marriage, we must face the thorny issues involved in the free will/predestination issue. We have seen what the will of God entails. What about the will of man? How do the two relate? How free is man, after all?

Chapter Two

THE MEANING OF MAN'S WILL

The term *free will* as applied to man is often glibly declared with little or no understanding of its meaning. There is actually no unified theory of man's free will, but a variety of competing and often conflicting views about it.

The question of man's free will is made more complicated by the fact that we must examine it in terms of how the will functioned before and after the fall of Adam. Most important is how the fall affected man's moral choices.

Augustine gave the church a close analysis of the state of freedom that Adam enjoyed before the fall. His classic concept of freedom distinguished four possibilities. In Latin, they are:

1. *posse pecarre*—able to sin
2. *posse non pecarre*—able not to sin (or to remain free from sin)
3. *non posse pecarre*—unable to sin
4. *non posse, non pecarre*—unable not to sin

Augustine argued that before the fall, Adam possessed both the ability to sin (*posse pecarre*) and the ability to not sin (*posse non pecarre*). However, Adam lacked the exalted state of the inability to sin that God enjoys (*non posse pecarre*). God's inability to sin is based not on an inner powerlessness to do what He wants, but rather on the fact that God has no inner desire to sin. Since the desire for sin is utterly absent from God, there is no reason for God to choose sin.

Before the fall, Adam did not have the moral perfection of God, but neither did he have the inability to refrain from sin (*non posse, non pecarre*). During his time of "probation" in the garden, he had the ability to sin and the ability not to sin. He chose to exercise the ability to sin and thus plunged the human race into ruin.

As a result, Adam's first sin was passed on to all his

descendants. Original sin refers not to the first sin but to God's punishment of that first transgression. Because of the first sin, human nature fell into a morally corrupt state, itself partly a judgment of God. When we speak of original sin, we refer to the fallen human condition that reflects the judgment of God on the race.

The Fallenness of Man

Christians differ in their views concerning the extent and seriousness of the fall. However, it is almost universally conceded that in dealing with mankind, we are dealing with a fallen race. Augustine located the depths of man's fallenness in his loss of original powers of righteousness. No longer does man have the ability to not sin. In man's fallen state, his plight is found in his inability to keep from sinning (*non posse, non pecarre*). In the fall, something profoundly vital to moral freedom was lost.

Augustine declared that in his prefallen state, man enjoyed both a free will (*liberium arbitrium*) and moral liberty (*libertas*). Since the fall, man has continued to have a free will, but has lost the moral liberty he once enjoyed.

Perhaps the most insightful study of the question of fallen man's free will is the epic work of Jonathan Edwards,

On the Freedom of the Will. Edwards and Augustine differ in terminology, but their meaning is essentially the same. Edwards distinguished between the *natural ability* of freedom and the *moral ability* of freedom. Natural ability deals with the powers of action and choice that we possess by nature. Man's natural abilities include the power to think, to walk, to speak, to eat, and so on. Man lacks the natural ability to fly, to live beneath the sea as a fish, or to hibernate for months without food. We may desire to fly, but we lack the natural equipment necessary to live out our desire. Our freedom has a certain built-in restriction related to the limitations of our natural faculties.

With respect to the making of choices, fallen man still has the natural ability and the natural faculties necessary to make moral choices. Man can still think, feel, and desire. All of the equipment necessary for the making of choices remains. What fallen man lacks is the moral disposition, the desire, or the inclination for righteousness.

Stated simply, man still has the ability to choose what he wants, but lacks the desire for true righteousness. He is *naturally free*, but he is *morally enslaved* to his own corrupt and wicked desires. Both Edwards and Augustine said man is still free to choose, but if left to himself, man will never choose righteousness, precisely because he does not desire it.

Edwards took the question a step further. He said man still has not only the ability but the built-in *necessity* to choose according to his desires. Not only *can* we choose what we want, we *must* choose what we want. It is at this point that the protest is sounded: Is free choice an illusion? If we *must* choose what we choose, how can such a choice be called *free*? If we are free to choose what we want but want only what is evil, how can we still speak of free will? This is precisely why Augustine distinguished between free will and liberty, saying that fallen man still has free will but has lost his liberty. It is why Edwards said that we still have natural freedom but have lost moral freedom.

Why talk of freedom at all, if we can choose only sin? The crux of the matter lies in the relationship between choice and desire, or disposition. Edwards's thesis is that we always choose according to the strongest inclination, or disposition, of the moment. Again, not only *can* we choose according to our strongest desires, we *must* choose according to our strongest desires of the moment. Such is the essence of freedom—that I am able to choose what I want when I want it.

If I *must* do something, then in a sense my actions are determined. But if my actions are determined, how can I be free? The classic answer to this difficult question is

CAN I KNOW GOD'S WILL?

that the determination of my choices comes from within me. The essence of freedom is *self-determination*. It is when my choices are forced on me by external coercion that my freedom is lost. To be able to choose what I want by virtue of self-determination does not destroy free will but establishes it.

Choices Flow from Desires

To choose according to the strongest desire or inclination of the moment simply means that there is a reason for the choices I make. At one point, Edwards defined the will as "the mind choosing." The actual choice is an effect or result that requires an antecedent cause. The cause is located in the disposition or desire. If all effects have causes, then all choices likewise have causes. If the cause is apart from me, then I am a victim of coercion. If the cause is from within me, then my choices are self-determined or free.

Think about Edwards's thesis that we always choose according to the strongest inclination or desire of the moment. Think, if you will, of the most harmless choice that you might make in the course of a day. Perhaps you attend a meeting of a group and choose to sit on the left side in the third seat from the end of the fourth row at the front of the room. Why did you choose to sit there? In all probability, when you entered the room, you did not engage in a thorough analysis of your seating preferences. You probably did not make a chart to determine which seat was best. Your decision probably was made quickly, with little or no conscious evaluation and with a sense of apparent spontaneity. Does that mean, however, that there was no reason for your choice? Perhaps you sat where you did because you are comfortable sitting on the left side of the room in such meetings. Perhaps you were attracted to that seat because of its proximity to a friend or its access to the exit. In situations like this, the mind weighs a host of contributing factors so quickly that we tend to think our responses are spontaneous. The truth is that something in you triggered a desire to sit in a certain seat, or else your choice was an effect without a cause.

Perhaps your seat selection was governed by forces outside your control. Perhaps the seat you chose was the only seat left in the room, so that you had no choice in the matter at all. Is that completely true? The option to stand at the back of the room was still there. Or the option to leave the meeting altogether was still there. You chose to sit in the only seat available because your desire to sit was stronger than your desire to stand and your desire to stay was stronger than your desire to leave.

Consider a more bizarre illustration. Suppose on the way home from the meeting you encounter a robber who points a gun to your head and says, "Your money or your life." What do you do? If you accede to his demand and turn over your wallet, you will become a victim of coercion, and yet in some measure you will have exercised free choice. Coercion enters by virtue of the fact that the gunman is severely restricting your options to two. The element of freedom that is preserved stems from the fact that you still have two options and that you choose the one for which you have the strongest desire at the moment.

All things being equal, you have no desire to donate your money to an unworthy thief. You have even less desire, however, to have your brain poured out on the sidewalk by the gunman's bullet. Given the small number of options, you still choose according to the strongest inclination at the moment. We always do what we really want to do.

The Bible teaches, some will say, that we do not always do what we want to do. The apostle Paul lamented in Romans 7 that the good he wanted to do he did not do, and the thing he did not want to do was the very thing he did. Paul's frustration over the wretchedness of his condition would seem totally to refute Edwards's thesis of the relationship of choice to desire. Paul, however, was not giving expression to an analysis of the causal relationship between desire and choice. He was expressing a profound frustration that centers on the complex of desires that assault the human will.

We are creatures with a multitude of desires, many of which are in violent conflict with each other. Again, consider the "all things being equal" dimension of our moral choices. As a Christian I have a profound desire to please Christ with my life and to attain righteousness. That good desire for obedience to God is neither perfect nor pure, as it struggles daily with other desires in my sinful personality. If I had no conflicting desires, I would never be disobedient. If the only desire I had, or if the strongest desire I had, was to obey God continuously, I would never willfully sin against Him. However, there are times when my desire to sin is greater than my desire to obey; when that happens, I sin. When my desire to obey is greater than my desire to sin, at that moment I refrain from sinning. My choices reveal more clearly and more certainly than anything else the level of my desire.

Desire, like appetite, is not constant. Our levels of desire fluctuate from day to day, from hour to hour, and from minute to minute. Desire moves in an ebb-and-flow pattern like the waves of the sea. The person who goes on a diet experiences intensifying pangs of hunger at various times of the day. It is easy to make a resolution to diet when one is satiated. Likewise, it is easy to resolve to be righteous in the midst of a moving spiritual experience of prayer. Yet we are creatures of changing moods and fleeting desires who have not yet achieved a constancy of will based on a consistency of godly desires. As long as conflict of desire exists and an appetite for sin remains in the heart, man is not totally free in the moral sense of which Edwards spoke, and neither does he experience the fullness of liberty described by Augustine.

Choice as a Spontaneous Act

Over against the Augustinian view of free will is the classical notion that describes the action or activity of choice in purely spontaneous terms. In this concept, the will chooses and is free from not only external forces of coercion but from any internal rule of disposition or desire. The choice of the moment proceeds freely in the sense that no inclination or prior disposition controls, directs, or affects the choice that is made. It is safe to say that this is the dominant view of free will in Western culture and is the view Calvin had in mind when he stated, "Free will is far too grandiose a term to apply to man." At bottom it implies that man can make choices that are effects without any causes. Here it is suggested that the power of man to produce an effect without a cause exceeds even the creative power of God Almighty. Moreover, the cardinal rule of causality—*ex nihilo, nihil fit* ("out of nothing, nothing comes")—is broken. Such a view of freedom is repugnant not only to Scripture but to reason.

To understand freedom as purely spontaneous choice with no prior disposition controlling it is to rob freedom of any moral significance. That is, if I act with no prior motive or no previous inclination toward or away from righteousness, how can it be said that my act is moral at all? Such activity would be without reason or motive behind it; it would be a purely random action, with no moral virtue attached to it.

However, a deeper question remains: Is such a spontaneous action possible at all? If the will is inclined neither to the right nor to the left, how could it choose at all? If there is no disposition toward, or away from, the action, then the will suffers from complete paralysis. It is like the donkey that had set before him a bale of hay and a bucket of oats. The donkey's inclination with respect to the hay and the oats was exactly equal, with not the slightest degree of preference toward one or the other. The story is told that the donkey in such circumstances starves to death with a banquet feast in front of him because he has no way to choose between the two.

The practical problem that remains with the classical view of freedom is one raised by behavioristic psychology. If man is indeed self-determined or free, does that not imply that if his desires were completely known, man's action in every given circumstance would be completely predictable? There is a sense in which we must agree that such a predictability would be implied. However, there is no way that any genius short of God and His omniscience could possibly know all the complex factors present in the human mind weighing a choice.

We recognize with psychologists that preferences and inclinations are shaped in many respects by experience and environment, but we cannot predict with certainty what any human being will do. Hidden variables within the complex of human personality make for this unpredictability. It nevertheless remains a fact that there is always a reason for our actions, a cause for our choices. That cause stems partly from ourselves and partly from the forces operating around and over against us.

The Definition of Freedom

The safest course to steer is to define freedom as did the church fathers, such as Augustine: "the ability to choose what we want." God's sovereignty does not extinguish that dimension of human personality, but certainly rules over it.

Out of rigid forms of determinism comes the cry of despair: "If the complex factors that make up personality completely determine my choices, then what value is self-improvement or the search for righteousness? If my will is enslaved by my dispositions and desires, what hope do I have of ever breaking out of the patterns of sin that are so destructive to my present mode of behavior?"

In a real sense, the process of sanctification involves a radical reprogramming of the inner self. We are not the victims of blind mechanical forces that control our destiny. As intelligent beings, we can do something to change the dispositions of our hearts and the inclinations of our minds.

It is important to remember that desire is not a fixed and constant power that beats within our souls. Our desires change and fluctuate from moment to moment. When the Bible calls us to feed the new man and starve the old man, we can apply this injunction by taking advantage of the ebb and flow of moods to strengthen the new man when our desire for Christ is inflamed and to kill the old man's desires by starving him in times of satiation. The simplest way to state the mechanism of sin is to understand that at the moment I sin, I desire the sin more than I desire to please God. Stated another way, my love for the sin is greater at the moment of its intense desire than is my love for obedience to God. Therefore, the simple conclusion is that to overcome the power of sin within us, we need either to decrease our desire for the sin or to increase our desire to obey God.

What can we do to effect such changes? We can submit ourselves to the discipline of a class or a teacher and devote ourselves to a rigorous study of the law of God. Such disciplined study can help renew our minds, equipping us with a new understanding of what pleases and displeases God. The development of a renewed mind is the biblical definition of spiritual transformation.

The mind and the will are linked, as Edwards noted. Understanding more deeply how abhorrent our sin is to God can change or reprogram our attitudes toward sin. We are to follow the biblical injunction to concentrate on whatever things are pure and good. It may be too much to expect that a man in the midst of an attack of profound lust will switch to pure thoughts. It would be difficult for him to push a button and change the inclination of his desire at that moment. However, in a more sober mood, he may have the opportunity to reprogram his mind by filling it with high and holy thoughts of the things of God. The end result is that he may well strengthen the disposition of his heart toward God and weaken the disposition of his fallen nature toward sin.

We need not surrender to a superficial form of rigid determinism or behaviorism that would cause us to despair of any hope of change. Scripture encourages us to work out our salvation "with fear and trembling," knowing that not only are we applying the means of grace by our own effort, but that God Himself is working within us to bring about the necessary changes to conform us to the image of His Son (Phil. 2:12–13; 1:6).

Sovereignty of God and Freedom of Man

What about man's will with respect to the sovereignty of God? Perhaps the oldest dilemma of the Christian faith is the apparent contradiction between the sovereignty of God and the freedom of man. If we define human freedom as *autonomy* (meaning that man is free to do whatever he pleases, without constraint, without accountability to the will of God), then of course we must say that free will is contradictory to divine sovereignty. We cannot soft-pedal this dilemma by calling it a mystery; we must face up to the full import of the concept. If free will means autonomy, then God cannot be sovereign. If man is utterly and completely free to do as he pleases, there can be no sovereign God. However, if God is utterly sovereign to do as He pleases, no creature can be autonomous.

It is possible to have a multitude of beings, all of whom are free to various degrees but none of whom are sovereign. The degree of freedom is determined by the level of power, authority, and responsibility held by each being. However, we do not live in this type of universe. There is a God who is sovereign—which is to say, He is absolutely free. My freedom is always within limits. My freedom is always constrained by the sovereignty of God. I have freedom to do things as I please, but if my freedom conflicts with the decretive will of God, there is no question as to the outcome—God's decree will prevail over my choice.

It is stated so often that it has become almost an uncritically accepted axiom within Christian circles that the sovereignty of God may never violate human freedom in the sense that God's sovereign will may never overrule human freedom. The thought verges on, if not trespasses, the border of blasphemy because it contains the idea that God's sovereignty is constrained by human freedom. If that were true, man, not God, would be sovereign, and God would be restrained and constrained by the power of human freedom. As I say, the implication here is blasphemous because it raises the creature to the stature of the Creator. God's glory, majesty, and honor are denigrated since He is reduced to the status of a secondary, impotent creature. Biblically speaking, man is free, but his freedom can never violate or overrule God's sovereignty.

I and my son are free moral agents; he has a will and I have a will. However, when he was a teen living in my home, his will was more often constrained by my will than was my will constrained by His. I carried more authority and more power in the relationship and hence I had a wider expanse of freedom than he had. So it is with our relationship to God; God's power and authority are infinite, and His freedom is never hindered by human volition.

There is no contradiction between God's sovereignty and man's free will. Those who see a contradiction, or even point to the problem as an unsolvable mystery, have misunderstood the mystery. The real mystery regarding free will is how it was exercised by Adam before the fall.

Options for Considering Adam's Sin

If Augustine was correct that pre-fall Adam possessed an ability to sin and an ability not to sin, and that he was created with no prior disposition or inclination toward sin, then the question we face is, "How was it possible for such a creature with no prior disposition toward evil actually to take the step into evil?" As we grapple with this mystery, let me present several options that have served as explanations in the past.

First, we can hypothesize that Adam fell because he was duped by the craftiness of Satan and simply did not know what he was doing. The inspiration for this hypothesis is the biblical emphasis on the craftiness of the Devil. Satan, in his guile, was able to seduce Adam and Eve by confusing their thought patterns. Thus, the weakness of our primordial parents was not moral in nature, but intellectual, inasmuch as they failed to perceive the chicanery of the serpent. What complicates the picture is the fact that the Scriptures in this instance do not describe Adam and Eve as having been completely duped by their adversary; rather, they had full knowledge of what God allowed and did not allow them to do. They could not plead ignorance of the command of God as an excuse for their transgression.

There are times when ignorance is excusable, namely when such ignorance cannot possibly be helped or overcome. Such ignorance is properly described by the Roman Catholic Church as "invincible ignorance"—ignorance that we lack the power to conquer. Invincible ignorance excuses and gives one a reprieve from any accusation of moral wrongdoing. However, the biblical record gainsays this option in the case of Adam and Eve, for God pronounces judgment on them. Unless that judgment was arbitrary or immoral on the part of God Himself, we can only conclude that what Adam and Eve did was inexcusable. A just God does not punish excusable transgressions. Indeed, *excusable* transgressions are not transgressions.

A second option is that Adam and Eve were coerced by Satan to disobey God. Here we see the original instance of the statement "The Devil made me do it." If, however, Satan, in fact, fully and forcibly coerced Adam and Eve to transgress the law of God, then once again we would find an excuse for their actions. We would have to conclude that they did not act with a reasonable measure of freedom, a measure that would at least have delivered them from moral culpability. Such a theory violates the clear teaching of the biblical text, which hints at no coercive manipulation on the part of Satan.

Consistently, the Scriptures place the responsibility, the blame, and the full culpability on Adam and Eve themselves. They committed evil. Their choice was an evil one.

By what means did Adam and Eve make an evil choice? If we apply the analysis of choice common to Augustine and Edwards to pre-fall Adam, we face an insoluble dilemma. If Adam had been created with a purely neutral disposition (with no inclination toward righteousness or evil), we would still face the same rational impasse that Edwards notes for those who would impose it for post-fall man. A will with no predisposition would have no motivation to choose. Without motivation, there could be no choice. Even if such a choice were possible, it would have no moral import to it.

We must examine the other two alternatives—that Adam was created with a predisposition toward evil or with a singular predisposition toward good. Both of these options end at the stone wall of intellectual difficulty. If we assume that Adam was created with a predisposition toward evil, we cast a horrible shadow over the character of God, for this would mean that God created man with a predisposition toward evil and then punished man for exercising the disposition that God Himself had planted within his soul. In a real sense, this would make God the author of, and the one ultimately responsible for, human wickedness.

Every page of Holy Scripture recoils from such a thesis, as it would transfer the blame from man to God Himself, who is altogether good. Still, many take this option, following in the footsteps of the implied criticism of the first man, Adam, who excused himself before the Creator by saying, "The woman whom *you* gave to be with me, she gave me fruit of the tree, and I ate" (Gen. 3:12, emphasis added). Men from Adam onward have manifested their fallenness by trying to transfer the blame for that fallenness to the Creator.

A third option is that God created man with a disposition toward only righteousness. If this were the case, then we have an effect without a sufficient cause. How is it possible for a creature created with the disposition toward only righteousness to have chosen a wicked act?

Other Inquiries into the Mystery of Adam's Sin

I have a built-in antipathy to dialectical theology—theology that proclaims the beauty of contradictions and nonsense statements. Thus, I must swallow hard to agree with one neoorthodox theologian about the origin of Adam's sin. Karl Barth calls the sin of Adam the "impossible possibility." Barth, of course, is calling attention to the utterly inexplicable mystery of Adam's transgression—what was rationally impossible and inconceivable happened, and remains a bona fide and impenetrable mystery to us.

Other attempts have been made to seek a complex and sophisticated answer to the mystery of iniquity. One suggestion is that the sin of Adam was like all sin, namely, a privation, a corruption, or a negation of something that was inherently and intrinsically good. In other words, Adam was created with a good moral disposition. His appetites and desires were continuously good, and as a result, one would expect his activities to have been equally good. However, it is suggested that in the complexity of moral choices, sometimes a good will (which has a desire that in itself is good) can be misused and abused toward an evil end. The supreme example of such a twisting occurred at the temptation of Jesus, the second and new Adam.

In Jesus' temptation experience in the wilderness, Satan came to Him in the midst of a prolonged fast. It is probably safe to assume that at that point Jesus had a consuming passion for food. That natural human desire to eat carried no immoral overtones in and of itself. One expects a hungry man to have a disposition to eat. However, Jesus wanted to obey God through this act of self-deprivation. When Satan came to Jesus and suggested that He turn stones into bread, Satan was appealing to a perfectly normal appetite and desire within Jesus. However, Jesus' desire to obey the Father was deeper than His desire to partake of food. Thus, filled with an altogether righteous desire, He was able to overcome the temptation of Satan.

Now the theory goes like this: Perhaps it was something good that caused Adam to fall—something that in and of itself was good, but which could have been misused and abused by the seductive influences of Satan. Such an explanation certainly helps make the fall more understandable, but it goes only so far before it fails. At its most vital point, the explanation does not account for how this good desire could have become distorted, overruling the prior obligation to obey God. At some point before the act of transgression took place, Adam must have had to desire disobedience to God more than obedience to God; therein the fall already had taken place because the very desire to act against God in disobedience is itself sinful.

I leave the question of explaining the fall of Adam by virtue of the exercise of his free will to the hands of more competent and insightful theologians. To blame it on man's finite limitations is really putting blame on the God who made man finite. Biblically, the issue has been, and always will be, a moral one. Man was commanded by the Creator not to sin, but man chose to sin, though not because God or anyone else forced him. Man chose out of his own heart.

Consequently, to probe the answer to the *how* of man's sin is to enter the realm of deepest mystery. Perhaps all we can do in the final analysis is to recognize the reality of our sin and our responsibility for it. Though we cannot explain it, certainly we know enough to confess it. We must never attribute the cause of our sin to God or adopt any position that would excuse us from the moral responsibility that Scripture clearly assigns to us.

Some have criticized the Christian faith for its inability to give a satisfying answer to the question of sin. The fact is that other religions must come to terms with this same question. Some respond simply by denying the reality of evil—a convenient but absurd way out. Christianity alone deals head-on with the reality of sin by providing an escape from its consequences.

The Christian solution to the problem of sin is a radical departure from what other religions provide, for it is centered in the person and work of Jesus Christ. Through His perfect sacrifice, which has the efficacy of blotting out believers' sins, we have become righteous in God's eyes. However, that righteousness does not give us the license to do as we please. We must still seek to do God's preceptive will, especially as we swim through the perilous waters of the moral, ethical, and social dilemmas of our age.

While we have discussed the more theological aspects of man's will and God's will, two other topics now beckon us: God's will for our jobs and for our marital status. These two practical concerns take center stage in the drama of our personal lives. What can we learn about God's will and man's will in relation to these vital aspects of living? The next chapters offer guidelines to facilitate our decision making in these all-important areas.

Chapter Three

GOD'S WILL
AND YOUR JOB

When we are introduced to people, the following three questions are generally asked: "What is your name?" "Where are you from?" and "What do you do?" The third question is the one that concerns us in this chapter.

"What do you do?" is obviously a question about one's occupation, career, or vocation. People want to know what task or service constitutes our livelihood or helps fulfill our personal aspirations.

We are all familiar with the aphorism, "All work and no

play makes Jack a dull boy." We understand that life is more than work. We devote periods of time to recreation, sleep, play, and other activities not directly part of our principal employment or labor. However, the portion of our lives that is taken up by work is so encompassing and time-consuming that we tend to understand our personal identity in the light of our work.

Whatever else we are, we are creatures involved in labor. This was the design of creation—God Himself is a working God. From the very moment of creation, He conferred on our original parents the responsibilities of work. Adam and Eve were called to dress, till, and keep the earth, to name the animals, and to have dominion by way of managerial responsibility over the earth. All of these activities involved the expenditure of time, energy, and resources—in short, work.

Sometimes we fall into the trap of thinking that work is a punishment that God gave us as a result of Adam's fall in the Garden of Eden. We must remember that work was given *before* the fall. To be sure, our labor has additional burdens attached to it because of the fall. A mixture of thorns and thistles is found among the good plants we seek to cultivate. Our labor is accomplished by the sweat of our brow. These were some of the penalties of sinfulness, but work itself was part of the glorious privilege granted to men and women in creation. It is impossible to understand our own humanity without understanding the central importance of work.

Most of us spend the early years of our lives preparing and training for a lifelong activity of work. The sensitive Christian understands that in the labor of his occupation, he is responsible to make a contribution to the kingdom of God, to fulfill a divine mandate, to embark on a holy calling as a servant of the living God. Such a Christian is keenly interested to discover how best to serve God through his labor.

Vocation and Calling

The idea of vocation is based on the theological premise of a divine call. The word *vocation* comes from the Latin word meaning "calling." In our secular society, the religious meaning of the term has lost its significance, having become merely a synonym for *career*. I will be using the term *vocation* in its original sense: a divine call, a holy summons to fulfill a task or a responsibility that God has laid on us. The question we as Christians wrestle with is, "Am I in the center of God's will with respect to my vocation?" In other words, "Am I doing with my life what God wants me to do?" Here the question of the will of God becomes eminently practical, for it touches on that dimension of my life that fills most of my waking hours and has the greatest impact on the shaping of my personality.

If the Bible teaches anything, it teaches that God is a calling God. The world was created through the call of the omnipotent Creator: "'Let there be light,' and there was light" (Gen. 1:1). God also calls His people to repentance, to conversion, and to membership in His family. In addition, He calls us to serve Him in His kingdom, making the best possible use of our gifts and talents. Still, the question faces us: "How do I know what is my particular vocational calling?"

One of the great tragedies of modern society is that, although the job market is vast and complex with an infinite number of possible careers, the educational systems that train us tend to guide and direct us to a very small number of occupational choices. When I was a high school graduate embarking on college, a great deal of discussion centered on one's major and career aspirations. At that time, it seemed as if everyone was setting out to become an engineer. The mechanized culture of the 1950s was opening up thousands of lucrative positions in engineering. College campuses were flooded with young aspirants for degrees in the field of engineering.

I also remember the engineer glut on the market that occurred in the 1970s. Stories circulated about people with doctorates in engineering who were collecting unemployment or washing dishes in the local diner because there simply were not enough engineering jobs available. The same could be said for education majors. Positions in education became fewer and fewer while the number of applicants became greater and greater. The problem was heightened by misguided publicity and counseling that steered people into occupational roles that society already had filled.

In the early twentieth century, the choices were much less difficult since the vast majority of American children spent their time preparing for a life in agricultural labor. Today, roughly two percent of the population is employed in farming—a radical decrease in one occupation that has opened the door for a vast number of other occupations.

Finding Your Vocation

The question of vocation becomes a crisis at two major points in life. The first is in late adolescence, when a person is pressured into deciding what skills and knowledge he should acquire for future use. Some college freshmen feel pressured to declare a major in their first year, before knowing the available options and the limits of their ability.

The second period in life when vocation becomes critical is in midlife, when a person experiences a sense of frustration, failure, or lack of fulfillment in his current position. He may ask: "Have I wasted my life? Am I sentenced forever to a job that I'm finding meaningless, unfulfilling, and frustrating?" Such questions highlight the fact that vocational counseling is a major part of pastoral counseling in America, second only to marital counseling.

We must also consider the fact that vocational frustration is a major contributing cause of marital disharmony and family strife. Thus, it is important to approach the matter of vocation with great care, both in the early stages of adolescent development and in the latter stages, when the sense of frustration hits home.

The problem of discerning one's calling focuses heavily on four important questions:

1. What *can* I do?
2. What do I *like* to do?
3. What would I like to be *able* to do?
4. What *should* I do?

The last question can plague the sensitive conscience. To begin to answer it, we need to take a look at the other three questions because they are closely linked to the ultimate question, "What should I do?"

What can I do? Reasonably assessing our abilities, skills, and aptitudes is a crucial and basic part of the decision-making process in choosing a vocation. We need to ask: "What are my abilities? What am I equipped to do?"

We may object that Moses and Jeremiah both protested against God's call by saying that they were not equipped for the task. Moses protested that he had limited speaking ability, and Jeremiah reminded his Creator of his youthfulness. Both experienced God's rebuke for seeking to evade a divine calling on the basis of the flimsy claim that they lacked the ability to do the job.

Neither Moses nor Jeremiah had a full understanding of what was needed to carry out the summons God gave him. Moses, for instance, protested that he lacked speaking skill, but God had prepared Aaron to help Moses with that part of the task. What God was looking for was obedient leadership from Moses; public speaking could be delegated to another. God certainly took into consideration Moses' gifts, abilities, and aptitude before He called him.

We must remember that God is the perfect Manager.

He is efficient in His selection, calling people according to the gifts and talents that He has given them. Satan's strategy is to manipulate Christians into positions for which they have no ability or skill to perform well. Satan himself is very efficient in directing Christians to inefficiency and ineffectiveness.

What can I do? This question can be answered by proficiency examinations, analysis of our strengths and weaknesses, and a sober evaluation of our past performance. Abilities and performances can be, and are, measured in sophisticated ways in our society. We need to know the parameters of our abilities.

People often apply for positions for which they have no skill. This is particularly and sadly true within the church and in related Christian service. Some hunger and thirst to be in full-time Christian service but lack the ability and the gifts required for the particular job. For example, they may have the academic training and credentials for the pastorate, but lack the managerial skills or the people skills to be effective pastors.

Perhaps the most important principle in Scripture regarding abilities is found in Paul's injunction that we ought to make a sober analysis of ourselves, not thinking too highly of ourselves (Rom. 12:3). Through sober analysis, we can make a serious, honest, and clear evaluation of what we can and cannot do, and we should act accordingly.

The young person has a different question: What would I *like* to be able to do? Such a person may have developed very few skills or have little educational background, but he realizes that he has enough time to acquire skills and talents through education or vocational training.

At this point, the concept of aptitude is relevant. Aptitude involves a person's latent abilities as well as his acquired abilities. A person may have a certain aptitude for mechanical things and have no aptitude whatsoever for abstract things. This person may desire to be a philosopher but would make a far better investment of his time by learning to be an airplane mechanic. However, preferences are still important. Here we tread into that critical and frightening area of human experience called the realm of motivation.

Motivated Abilities

Research indicates that most people have more than one ability, and that their abilities can be divided into two basic types: *motivated* abilities and *non-motivated* abilities. A non-motivated ability is a skill or a strength that a person has but is not motivated to use. Some people are very good at doing certain things, but find no particular fulfillment or enjoyment in doing them. Performing them is sheer drudgery and pain. They may be proficient in what they do, but for one reason or another they find the task odious.

I know of one young woman who in her early teenage years attracted national attention because of her proficiency at the game of golf. While still a teenager, she won a national tournament. Yet when the time came for girls her age to turn professional, she chose a different vocation, not out of a higher calling to seek a more spiritual enterprise than professional athletics, but because she found golf to be very unpleasant. Her displeasure came as the result of fierce pressure her father had placed on her in pushing her to become a proficient golfer at a young age. When she became of age and was out from under parental authority, she decided to do something else. She had the ability to become a professional golfer, but she lacked the motivation.

We might ask, "How could she have become so proficient in the first place if she had not been motivated to perform well in golf?" We have to realize that she had been motivated to become proficient, but the motivation was largely based on fear of her father's wrath. In order to please him, she disciplined herself to acquire a skill that she never would have pursued on her own. Once free from the driving force of his authority, she turned her vocational pursuits in another direction. The moral to the story is obvious. The person who gives his full measure of time and energy to a non-motivated ability is a walking pressure cooker of frustration.

It is true that, as Christians, we don't always have the luxury of doing the things we want to do. God calls us to sacrifice and to be willing to participate in the humiliation of Christ. To be sure, we live in the midst of warfare, and as Christians we have signed up for the duration. We should never neglect our awesome responsibility to the kingdom of God. Called to be servants, we are also called to obedience. Sometimes we are called to do things that we don't particularly enjoy doing. Nevertheless, the overriding consideration is to bring our motivation into conformity with our call and our call into conformity with our motivation.

All things being equal, Jesus did not want to go to the cross, as He expressed in His agony in the Garden of Gethsemane. Yet at the same time, He had an overarching desire and motivation to do the will of His Father. That was His "meat and drink," the focus of His zeal. When it was confirmed to Him that it was the Father's will that He lay down His life, Jesus was, in a very real and vital sense, motivated to do it.

Let us extend the concept of service and obedience to the analogy of human warfare. A crisis besets a nation, and people are summoned to the cause of national defense. Leaving the security and comfort of their homes and jobs, they make sacrifices by enlisting in the armed services. Are not Christians called to do the same? Certainly there is a sense in which we are. Yet within the context of the earthly military, there are a vast number of jobs, some for which we would be suited and others for which we would not. Some military tasks would be in line with our motivated skills and patterns of behavior, while others would be completely at odds with our motivated skills and behavior. Even within the context of sacrificial service, a consideration of motivation is a vital ingredient in determining our vocation.

Some rugged individualists in our society are self-employed and find it totally unnecessary to fit into an organizational working structure that involves supervisors, bosses, and lines of authority. Most of us, however, carry out our working lives within the context of an organization. Here we face the problem of *fitting*. Do our jobs fit our gifts, talents, and aspirations? Do our motivated abilities fit our jobs? The degree to which our job requirements and our motivated abilities fit often determines the usefulness of our contribution and the extent of our personal satisfaction.

When personal motivations do not fit job descriptions, many people suffer. The first to suffer is the individual, because he is laboring in a job that does not fit his motivated abilities. Because he is in a job for which he is unsuited, he tends to be less efficient and less productive. He also creates problems for others in the organization because his frustration spills over and has a negative effect on the group.

Some of us are "sanctified" enough to perform assigned tasks for which we lack motivation, doing them as proficiently as we do tasks that are more enjoyable. However, people who are that sanctified make up an infinitesimal minority within the workforce. Research shows again and again that there is a strong tendency for people to do what they are motivated to do, regardless of what is called for in their job description. That is, they spend the majority of their time and effort doing what they want to do rather than what the job, in fact, calls them to do. Such an investment of time and energy can be quite costly to a company or an organization.

The following simple diagrams show the relationships between motivated ability patterns and job descriptions. They have been borrowed from People Management, a Connecticut-based organization. People Management helps people to discern their motivated ability patterns and helps organizations to coordinate people's gifts and motivations with the needs and aims of the organizations. This kind of guidance works not only in secular industry but also within the structures of the church and sacred vocations.

MISFIT DIAGRAM

Job Description		Unused Abilities
Tasks Not Performed		Motivated Abilities

Personal Frustration (right side, vertical)

Organizational Frustration (left side, vertical)

Job Fit

In this diagram, the top left block represents the job description of the employee, including the tasks required for optimal organizational functioning.

The lower right block represents the motivated abilities of the employee. The shaded area represents the area of job fit. It is not in balance. A large portion of the employee's motivated abilities are not being used. This produces frustration for the employee.

Also, a large portion of the organizational job description is either left unperformed or performed at a low degree of proficiency. The result is organizational frustration. This pattern spells problems for both the individual employee and the organization. Changes must be made.

The diagram below represents an ideal matchup between job description and motivated abilities. The result is fulfillment for both the employee and the organization.

ORGANIZATIONAL FIT

Through the influence of the world-denying spirit of Manichaeism, early Christians got the idea that the only way they could possibly serve God would be by living their lives on a bed of nails. It was assumed that to embark on a pathway of service involved self-denial. Real virtue could be found only in being as miserable as possible in one's job. However, if God indeed called us to devote ourselves to the most unpleasant tasks possible, He would be the cosmic Chief of Bad Managers.

The Scriptures describe God's management style differently. God manages by building us into a body according to our abilities and our desires. He gives gifts to each one of His people. Every Christian is gifted of the Lord to fulfill a divine vocation. Along with the gift, God gives a desire or a motivation to make use of that gift.

What Should We Do?

This brings us to the final and paramount question: "What *should* I do?" The most practical advice I can give is for you to do what your motivated ability pattern indicates you can do with a high degree of motivation. If what you would like to do can be of service to God, then by all means you should be doing it.

One vital constraint is at work: the preceptive will of God. If a woman's great ability and motivation were to be a prostitute and a man's motivated ability were to be the world's greatest bank robber, then obviously vocational goals would have to be adjusted. To fulfill such motivated abilities would bring individuals into direct conflict with the preceptive will of God.

If we carefully analyzed the root causes for the motivated ability of the bank robber and the motivated ability of the prostitute, we probably would find root abilities and motivations that could profitably and productively be channeled into godly enterprises. We must not only bring our motivated abilities into conformity with the law of God, but also make sure that the vocation we choose has the blessing of God.

There is certainly nothing wrong, for example, with devoting one's life to the practice of medicine, for we see the good that medicine can do in terms of alleviating suffering. We also understand that the world needs bread to eat and that the vocation of baker for someone who is motivated and able to bake is a godly enterprise. Jesus Himself spent many of His years not in preaching and teaching but in being a carpenter, a craftsman in a legitimate trade. During those years, Jesus was in "the center of God's will."

Any vocation that meets the need of God's world can be considered a divine calling. I underscore this because of the tendency in Christian circles to think that only those who go into "full-time Christian service" are being sensitive to divine vocation—as if preaching and teaching were the only legitimate tasks to which God calls us. A cursory reading of the Bible would reveal the flaw in such thinking. The temple was built in the Old Testament through not only the wise oversight of Solomon but also the craftsmanship of those who were divinely gifted in carving, sculpting, and so on.

David's vocation as a shepherd, Abraham's vocation as a caravan trader, Paul's vocation as a tentmaker—all were seen as part of God's plan to bring about the redemption of the world. When God made Adam and Eve, neither was called to be a full-time professional worker in the ecclesiastical structure; they were basically called to be farmers.

A vocation is something that we receive from God; He is the one who calls us. He may not call us in the way that He called Moses, by appearing in a burning bush and giving a specific set of marching orders. Instead, He usually calls us inwardly and by giving us certain gifts, talents, and aspirations. His invisible sovereign will is certainly working in the background to prepare us for useful tasks in His vineyard.

The External Call from People

In addition to the inner call of God, we recognize that there is such a thing as an external call to labor, a call that comes from people who request our services for their particular mission or purpose. We may be called by the church to be preachers or by a company to be foremen or shippers. Every time an organization places a want ad in a newspaper, a human call is going out for able workers to come and match their gifts and talents to a presented need.

Some Christians have argued that the need always constitutes the call. They say that there is a need for evangelists in the world and therefore everyone should be an evangelist. I agree that we must consider the needs of the kingdom of God as we make vocational decisions. However, the very fact that the world needs evangelists does not necessarily imply that everyone in the world is called to be an evangelist. Again, the New Testament makes it clear that not all are called to be preachers or administrators. The church is composed of people with a diversity of gifts, talents, and vocations. We must not make a simplistic, passive assumption that the need constitutes the call.

Certainly the presence of a need requires that the people of God strive to meet that need. However, it does not necessarily mean that people who are not equipped to meet the need are thereby forced into the gap. For example, it is every Christian's responsibility to help carry out the mandate for evangelism. It is not every Christian's responsibility to be an evangelist. I am not an evangelist, though I contribute to evangelism by teaching evangelists theology and by contributing money for the church's task of evangelism. I do those things so that those who do have the gift and the motivation can be called out, trained, equipped, and sent into the world as evangelists. I participate in the responsibility of the body of Christ to see that the task is met, but I myself am not the one who delivers the goods as the practicing evangelist. I could say the same regarding a host of other vocations.

How do others affect our vocational calling? We do need to listen to the community of believers and friends. Sometimes our gifts and abilities are more evident to those around us than they are to us. The counsel of many and the evaluation of the group are important considerations in our search for our vocations. However, we must put up a red flag of warning. The group's judgment is not always correct. The fact that a particular individual or group thinks we should be doing a certain task is not a guarantee that it is the will of God.

I went through a period in my life of being unemployed for six months. During that time, I had five different job offers in five different cities in the United States. Five different friends came to me and said out of sincerity and urgent zeal that they were sure God wanted me to take each of the particular jobs. This meant that if all five of them had a direct pipeline to the will of God, God wanted me to hold five full-time positions and live in five different cities in the

United States at the same time. I explained to my friends that I knew I was iniquitous (full of sin), but had not yet discovered the gift of being ubiquitous (being everywhere at the same time). I simply could not possibly do all five jobs. Somebody was wrong in their estimation of the will of God for my life.

I find it very difficult to resist the pressures that come from people who are sure they know what God wants me to do with my life. We all experience that kind of pressure, so we must be careful to pay attention to those whose judgment we trust. We must be able to discern between sound judgment and the vested personal interests of other people.

As it turned out, I accepted a sixth position for which no one came to me in the middle of the night with a telegram from God. I was convinced that the sixth position was the one that matched my abilities with the job that needed to be done.

Considering Foreseeable Consequences

One last consideration that is often neglected but is of crucial importance is the foreseeable consequences of the job. To take a job simply for money or for geographical location is a tragic mistake. All things being equal, I would like to have a salary of a $1 million a year, to be a teacher of theology, and to live where the climate is mild twelve months of the year. At the present time I am a teacher of theology living in Florida, but I make far less than $1 million a year. Somewhere along the way, I had to make a decision about my priorities. Did I want to make a million dollars or did I want to heed my vocational calling? My residence was determined by the locale of my vocation.

Job decisions have both short-range and long-range consequences. Consider the case of Abraham and his nephew Lot, who lived and worked together in the Promised Land. Conflict between their hired hands made it necessary for them to divide the territory they were occupying. Abraham gave Lot the first choice, offering any half that he chose. Lot gazed toward the barren area of Transjordan and then looked toward the fertile valley near the city. He thought for a moment: "If I take the fertile valley, my cows can graze there and become fat. It's a short distance to the city market. My profit will be great." In consideration of his business, Lot opted for the fertile areas around the city and left Abraham the barren land. Lot's choice was brilliant—from the perspective of raising cattle. He didn't ask himself, "Where will my family go to school? Where will my family go to church?" The city he chose was Sodom—a great place to raise cows. The short-term consequences were fine, but long-term living in Sodom turned out to be a disaster in many ways.

How will our job decisions be conducive to fulfilling our other responsibilities? The person who chooses a vocation purely on the basis of money, location, or status is virtually guaranteeing his later frustration.

Much of the confusion we often experience in the job arena would be dispelled by asking ourselves one simple question: "What would I most like to do if I didn't have to please anyone in my family or my circle of friends?" Another good question is, "What would I like to be doing ten years from now?" These questions are good to keep in mind even after one has settled into a particular job. Another thing to remember is the promise of God's Word that the Holy Spirit will guide us into all truth. As His children, that includes the area of our work.

While God's decretive will may not always be clear to us even in our occupational pursuits, His preceptive will is more easily discerned. Wherever we are, in whatever work we find ourselves, His preceptive will must be done.

Finally, what does God expect of us in relation to our work? As Christians, we have been called to be spiritual salt in a decaying world, to be spiritual light in the midst of darkness. We are to be wise stewards of God's gifts and talents. That means striving to be the most honest, patient, hardworking, and committed workers we can be. It means settling for nothing less than excellence. God help us to live up to His high call for each of us.

Chapter Four

GOD'S WILL IN
MARRIAGE

Besides our work, the other topic of perennial concern is our marital status. Should we marry or remain single?

It is possible that Christians expend more decision-making energy over the subject of marriage than any other area of human existence. No wonder, since the decisions relevant to the marital relationship have such far-reaching effects on our lives. How a person feels about his marital status determines, in large part, his sense of fulfillment, his productivity, and his self-image. The reality and the seriousness of the marital relationship are brought home when we realize that the one who knows us most intimately, the one before whom we are the most fragile and vulnerable, and the one who powerfully shapes and influences our lives is our marriage partner. That is why entering the marital relationship is not something anyone should undertake lightly.

Before we tackle the general question, "Is it God's will for me to marry?" several specific questions need to be considered.

Should I Get Married?

The answer to this question has often been assumed by our culture, at least until recent years. Even today, most of us absorb the idea while growing up that marriage is a natural and integral part of normal life. In many ways—from the fairy-tale characters Snow White and Prince Charming, the romantic plays of Shakespeare, and some mass media heroes and heroines—we receive signals that society expects us to be numbered among the married. Among individuals who fail to fulfill this cultural expectation, those of a more traditional mindset are left with the nagging feeling that perhaps something is wrong with them, that they are abnormal.

In earlier generations, if a young man reached the age of thirty without getting married, he was suspected of having homosexual tendencies. If a woman was still single by thirty, it was often tacitly assumed that she had some defect that made her unattractive as a marriage partner or had lesbian preferences. Such assumptions are by no means found in the Scriptures.

From a biblical perspective, the pursuit of celibacy (as Scripture expects for the unmarried) is a legitimate option in some instances. Under other considerations, it is viewed as a definite preference. Though we have our Lord's blessing on the sanctity of marriage, we also have His example of personal choice to remain celibate, obviously in submission to the will of God. Christ was celibate not because of a lack of the masculine traits necessary to make Him desirable as a life partner. Rather, His divine purpose obviated the destiny of marriage, making it crucial that He devote Himself entirely to the preparation of His bride, the church, for His future wedding.

The most important biblical instruction that we have regarding celibacy is given by the apostle Paul in a lengthy passage from 1 Corinthians:

> Now concerning the unmarried, I have no command
> of the Lord, but I give my opinion as one who by the

Lord's mercy is trustworthy. I think that in view of the present distress it is well for a person to remain as he is. Are you bound to a wife? Do not seek to be free. Are you free from a wife? Do not seek marriage. But if you marry, you do not sin, and if a girl marries she does not sin. Yet those who marry will have worldly troubles, and I would spare you that. I mean, brethren, the appointed time has grown very short; from now on, let those who have wives live as though they had none, and those who mourn as though they were not mourning, and those who rejoice as though they were not rejoicing, and those who buy as though they had no goods, and those who deal with the world as though they had no dealings with it. For the form of this world is passing away.

I want you to be free from anxieties. The unmarried man is anxious about the affairs of the Lord, how to please the Lord; but the married man is anxious about worldly affairs, how to please his wife, and his interests are divided. And the unmarried woman or girl is anxious about the affairs of the Lord, how to be holy in body and spirit; but the married woman is anxious about worldly affairs, how to please her husband. I say this for your own benefit, not to lay any restraint upon you, but to promote good order and to secure your undivided devotion to the Lord.

If anyone thinks that he is not behaving properly toward his betrothed, if his passions are strong, and it has to be, let him do as he wishes: let them marry—it is no sin. But whoever is firmly established in his heart, being under no necessity but having his desire under control, and has determined this in his heart, to keep her as his betrothed, he will do well. So that he who marries his betrothed does well; and he who refrains from marriage will do better.

A wife is bound to her husband as long as he lives. If the husband dies, she is free to be married to whom she wishes, only in the Lord. But in my judgment she is happier if she remains as she is. And I think that I have the Spirit of God. (1 Cor. 7:25–40, RSV)

Paul's teaching in this matter of marriage has been subjected to serious distortions. Some observe in this text that Paul is setting forth a contrasting view of marriage that says celibacy is good and marriage is bad, particularly for Christians called to service in the interim period between the first advent of Christ and His return. However, even a cursory glance at the text indicates that Paul is not contrasting the good and the bad, but rival goods. He points out that it is good to opt for celibacy under certain circumstances. Moreover, it is also good and quite permissible to opt for marriage under other circumstances. Paul sets forth the pitfalls that a Christian faces when contemplating marriage. Of prime consideration is the pressure of the kingdom of God on the marriage relationship.

Nowhere has the question of celibacy been more controversial than in the Roman Catholic Church. Historically, Protestants have objected that the Roman Catholic Church, by imposing on its clergy a mandate beyond the requirements of Scripture itself, has slipped into a form of legalism. Though we believe that Scripture permits the marriage of clergy, it indicates, at the same time, that one who is married and serving God in a special vocation does face the nagging problems created by a divided set of loyalties—his family on one hand, the church on the other. Unfortunately, the dispute between Protestants and Catholics over mandatory celibacy has become so heated at times that Protestants have often reacted to the other extreme, dismissing celibacy as a viable option. Let us return to the focus of Paul's word, which sets forth a distinction between rival goods. His distinction, in the final analysis, allows the individual to decide what best suits him or her.

Paul in no way denigrates the honorable "estate" of

marriage, but rather affirms what was given in creation: the benediction of God over the marriage relationship. One does not sin by getting married. Marriage is a legitimate, noble, and honorable option set forth for Christians.

Just a Piece of Paper?

Another aspect of the question, "Should I get married?" moves beyond the issue of celibacy to whether a couple should enter into a formal marriage contract or sidestep this option by simply living together. In the past few decades, the option of living together, rather than moving into a formal marriage contract, has proliferated in our culture. Christians must be careful not to establish their precepts of marriage (or any other ethical dimension of life) on the basis of contemporary community standards. The Christian's conscience is to be governed not merely by what is socially acceptable or even by what is legal according to the law of the land, but rather by what God sanctions.

Unfortunately, some Christians have rejected the legal and formal aspects of marriage, arguing that marriage is a matter of private and individual commitment between two people and has no legal or formal requirements. These view marriage as a matter of individual private decision apart from external ceremony. The question most frequently asked of clergymen on this matter reflects the so-called freedom in Christ: "Why do we have to sign a piece of paper to make it legal?"

The signing of a piece of paper is not a matter of affixing one's signature in ink to a meaningless document. The signing of a marriage certificate is an integral part of what the Bible calls a covenant. A covenant is made publicly before witnesses and with formal legal commitments that are taken seriously by the community. The protection of both partners is at stake; there is legal recourse should one of the partners act in a way that is destructive to the other.

Contracts are signed out of the necessity spawned by the presence of sin in our fallen nature. Because we have an enormous capacity to wound each other, sanctions have to be imposed by legal contracts. Contracts not only restrain sin, but also protect the innocent in the case of legal and moral violation. With every commitment I make to another human being, there is a sense in which a part of me becomes vulnerable, exposed to the response of the other person. No human enterprise renders a person more vulnerable to hurt than does the estate of marriage.

God ordained certain rules regulating marriage in order to protect people. His law was born of love, concern, and compassion for His fallen creatures. The sanctions God imposed on sexual activity outside marriage do not mean that God is a spoilsport or a prude. Sex is an enjoyment He Himself created and gave to the human race. God, in His infinite wisdom, understands that there is no time that human beings are more vulnerable than when they are engaged in this most intimate activity. Thus, He cloaks this special act of intimacy with certain safeguards. He is saying to both the man and the woman that it is safe to give oneself to the other only when there is a certain knowledge of a lifelong commitment behind it. There is a vast difference between a commitment sealed with a formal document and declared in the presence of witnesses, including family, friends, and authorities of church and state, and a whispered, hollow promise breathed in the back seat of a car.

Do I Want to Get Married?

Paul states in 1 Corinthians 7:8–9: "To the unmarried and the widows I say that it is good for them to remain single as I am. But if they cannot exercise self-control, they should marry. For it is better to marry than to burn with passion." The distinction is between the good and the better. Here Paul introduces the idea of burning, not of the punitive fires of hell, but of the passions of the biological nature, which God has given us. Paul is speaking very candidly when he points out that some people are not made for celibacy. Marriage is a perfectly honorable and legitimate option even for those who are most strongly motivated by sexual fulfillment and relief from sexual temptation and passion.

The question, "Do I want to get married?" is an obvious but very important one. The Bible does not prohibit marriage. Indeed, it encourages it except in certain cases where one may be brought into conflict with vocation, but even in that dimension, provisions are left for marriage. So to desire marriage is a very good thing. A person needs to be in touch with his own desires and conscience.

If I have a strong desire to marry, then the next step is to do something about fulfilling that desire. If a person wants a job, he must seriously pursue employment opportunities. When we decide to attend a college or a university, we have to follow the formal routine of making applications and evaluating various campuses. Marriage is no different; no magic recipe has come from heaven that will determine for us the perfect will of God for a life partner. Here, unfortunately, is where Christians have succumbed to the fairy-tale syndrome of our society. It is a particular problem for young, single women. Many a young woman feels that if God wants her to be married, He will drop a marriage partner out of heaven on a parachute or will bring some Prince Charming riding up to her doorstep on a great white horse.

One excruciating problem faced by single women— more so in past generations than today—is caused by the unwritten rule of our society that allows men the freedom actively to pursue a marriage partner while women are considered loose if they actively pursue a prospective husband. No biblical rule says that a woman eager to be married should be passive. There is nothing that prohibits her from actively seeking a suitable mate.

On numerous occasions, I've had the task of counseling single women who insisted at the beginning of the interview that they had no desire to be married but simply wanted to work out the dimensions of the celibacy they believed God had imposed on them. After a few questions and answers, the scenario usually repeats itself: the young woman begins to weep and blurts out, "But I really want to get married." When I suggest that there are wise steps that she can take to find a husband, her eyes light up in astonishment as if I had just given her permission to do the forbidden. I have broken a taboo.

Wisdom requires that the search be done with discretion and determination. Those seeking a life partner need to do certain obvious things, such as going where other single people congregate. They need to be involved in activities that will bring them in close communication with other single Christians.

In the Old Testament, Jacob made an arduous journey to his homeland to find a suitable marriage partner. He did not wait for God to deliver him a life partner. He went where the opportunity presented itself to find a marriage partner. But the fact that he was a man does not imply that such a procedure is limited to males. Women in our society have exactly the same freedom to pursue a mate by diligent search.

What Do I Want in a Marriage Partner?

A myth has arisen within the Christian community that marriage is to be a union between two people committed to the principle of selfless love. Selfless love is viewed as being crucial for the success of a marriage. This myth is based on the valid concept that selfishness is often at the root of disharmony and disintegration in marriage relationships. The biblical concept of love says no to acts of selfishness within marital and other human relationships. However, the remedy for selfishness is nowhere to be found in selflessness.

The concept of selflessness emerged from Asian and

Greek thinking, where the ideal goal of humanity is the loss of self-identity by becoming one with the universe. The goal of man in this schema is to lose any individual characteristic, becoming one drop in the great ocean. Another aspect of absorption is the notion of the individual becoming merged with the great Oversoul and becoming spiritually diffused throughout the universe. But from a biblical perspective, the goal of the individual is not the annihilation or the disintegration of the self, but the redemption of the self. To seek selflessness in marriage is an exercise in futility. The self is very active in building a good marriage, and marriage involves the commitment of the self with another self based on reciprocal sharing and sensitivity between two actively involved selves.

If I were committed to a selfless marriage, it would mean that in my search for a marriage partner I should survey the scene to find a person for whom I was willing to throw myself away. This is the opposite of what is involved in the quest for a marriage partner. When someone seeks a mate, he should be seeking someone who will enrich his life, who will add to his own self-fulfillment, and who at the same time will be enriched by that relationship.

What are the priority qualities to seek in a marriage partner? One little exercise that many couples have found helpful is based on freewheeling imagination. While finding a marriage partner is not like shopping for an automobile, one can use the new car metaphor. When one purchases a new car, he has many models from which to choose. With those models, there is an almost endless list of optional equipment that can be tacked onto the standard model.

By analogy, suppose one could request a made-to-order mate with all the options. The person engaged in such an exercise could list as many as a hundred qualities or characteristics that he would like to find in the perfect mate. Compatibility with work and with play, attitudes toward parenting, and certain skills and physical characteristics could be included. After completing the list, the person must acknowledge the futility of such a process. No human being will ever perfectly fit all the possible characteristics that one desires in a mate.

This exercise is particularly helpful for people who have delayed marrying into their late twenties or early thirties, or even later. Such a person sometimes settles into a pattern of focusing on tiny flaws that disqualify virtually every person he or she meets. After doing the made-to-order mate exercise, he can take the next step: reduce the list to the main priorities. The person involved in this exercise reduces the number of qualifications to twenty, then to ten, and finally to five. Such a reduction forces him to set in ordered priority the things he is most urgently seeking in a marriage partner.

It is extremely important that individuals clearly understand what they want out of the dating and eventually the marital relationship. They should also find out whether their desires in a marriage relationship are healthy or unhealthy. This leads us to the next question, regarding counseling.

From Whom Should I Seek Counsel?

Many people resent the suggestion that they seek counsel in their selection of a marriage partner. After all, isn't such a selection an intensely personal and private matter? However personal and private the decision might be, it is one of grave importance to the future of the couple and their potential offspring, their families, and their friends. Marriage is never ultimately a private matter, because how the marriage works affects a multitude of people. Therefore, counsel can and should be sought from trusted friends, pastors, and particularly from parents.

In earlier periods of Western history, marriages were arranged either by families or by matchmakers. Today, the idea of arranged marriages seems primitive and crass. It is totally foreign in the American culture. We have come to the place where we think that it is our inalienable right to choose one whom we love.

Some things need to be said in defense of the past custom of arranged marriages. One is that happy marriages can be achieved even when one has not chosen his own partner. It may sound outrageous, but I am convinced that if biblical precepts are applied consistently, virtually any two people in the world can build a happy marriage and honor the will of God in the relationship. That may not be what we prefer, but it can be accomplished if we are willing to work in the marital relationship. The second thing that needs to be said in defense of arranged marriages is that in some circumstances, marriages have been arranged on the objective evaluation of matching people together and of avoiding destructive parasitic matchups. For example, when left to themselves, people with significant personal weaknesses, such as a man with a profound need to be mothered and a woman with a profound need to mother, can be attracted to each other in a mutually destructive way. Such negative mergings happen daily in our society.

It is not my intention to lobby for matched or arranged marriages. I am only hailing the wisdom of seeking parental counsel in the decision-making process. Parents often object to the choice of a marriage partner. Sometimes their objections are based on the firm conviction that "no one is good enough for my daughter [or son]." Objections of this sort are based on unrealistic expectations at best and on petty jealousy at worst. However, not all parents are afflicted with such destructive prejudices regarding the potential marriage partners of their children. Sometimes the parents have keen insight into the personalities of their children, seeing blind spots that the offspring themselves are unable to perceive. In the earlier example of a person with an inordinate need to be mothered attracting someone with an inordinate need to mother, a discerning parent might spot the mismatch and caution against it. If a parent is opposed to a marriage relationship, it is extremely important to know why.

When Am I Ready to Get Married?

After seeking counsel, having a clear understanding of what we are hoping for, and having examined our expectations of marriage, the final decision is left to us. At this point, some face paralysis as the day of decision draws near. How does one know when he or she is ready to get married? Wisdom dictates that we enter into serious premarital study, evaluation, and counseling with competent counselors so that we may be warned of the pitfalls that come in this new and vital human relationship. With the breakdown of so many marriages in our culture, increasing numbers of young people fear entering into a marriage contract lest they become "statistics." Sometimes we need the gentle nudge of a trusted counselor to tell us when it is time to take the step.

What things need to be faced before taking the actual step toward marriage? Economic considerations are, of course, important. Financial pressures imposed on a relationship that is already besieged with emotional pressures of other kinds can be the straw that breaks the proverbial camel's back. That is why parents often advise young people to wait until they finish their schooling or until they are gainfully employed so that they can assume the responsibility of a family.

It is not by accident that the creation ordinance of marriage mentions that a man shall leave his father and mother and "hold fast to" his wife, and the two shall become "one flesh." The "leaving and cleaving" dimensions are rooted in the concept of being able to establish a new family unit. Here, economic realities often govern the preparedness for marriage.

Entering into marriage involves far more than embarking on new financial responsibilities. The marriage commitment is the most serious one that two human beings can make to each other. A person is ready to get married when he or she is prepared to commit to a particular person for the rest of his or her life, regardless of the human circumstances that befall them.

In order for us to understand the will of God for marriage, it is imperative that we pay attention to God's *preceptive will.* The New Testament clearly shows that God not only ordained marriage and sanctified it, He regulates it. His commandments cover a multitude of situations regarding the nitty-gritty aspects of marriage. The greatest textbook on marriage is sacred Scripture, which reveals God's wisdom and His rule governing the marriage relationship. If someone earnestly wants to do the will of God in marriage, his first task is to master what Scripture says that God requires in such a relationship.

What does God expect of His children who are married or thinking about getting married? God expects, among other things, faithfulness to the marriage partner, provision of mutual needs, and mutual respect under the lordship of Christ. Certainly the couple should enhance each other's effectiveness as Christians. If not, something is wrong.

While celibacy is certainly no less blessed and honorable a state than marriage, we have to recognize Adam and Eve as our models. God's plan involved the vital union of these two individuals who would make it possible for the earth to be filled with their "kind."

Basically, I cannot dictate God's will for anyone in this area any more than I can or would in the area of occupation. I will say that good marriages require hard work and individuals willing to make their marriages work.

What happens in our lives is cloaked ultimately in the mystery of God's will. The joy for us as His children is that the mystery holds no terror—only waiting, appropriate acting on His principles and direction, and the promise that He is with us forever.

About the Author

Dr. R. C. Sproul is the founder and chairman of Ligonier Ministries, an international multimedia ministry based in Lake Mary, Florida. He also serves as senior minister of preaching and teaching at Saint Andrew's in Sanford, Florida, and his teaching can be heard on the daily radio program *Renewing Your Mind*.

During his distinguished academic career, Dr. Sproul helped train men for the ministry as a professor at several leading theological seminaries.

He is the author of more than sixty books, including *The Holiness of God*, *Chosen by God*, *The Invisible Hand*, *Faith Alone*, *A Taste of Heaven*, *Truths We Confess*, *The Truth of the Cross*, and *The Prayer of the Lord*. He also served as general editor of *The Reformation Study Bible* and has written several children's books, including *The Prince's Poison Cup*.

Dr. Sproul and his wife, Vesta, make their home in Longwood, Florida.